Musical Instruments

This edition published 1978 by
Wayland (Publishers) Limited
49 Lansdowne Place, Hove, East Sussex BN3 1HF

781·91.

SBN 85340 529 8
© Sackett Publishing Services Ltd 1978

Filmset by Filmtype Services Limited, Scarborough
Printed in Italy by New Interlitho SpA

Beginning Crafts Series
Created and produced by Sackett Publishing Services Ltd
2 Great Marlborough Street London W1

Photography by Robert Glover Studios, Amersham, Bucks

Beginning Crafts

Musical Instruments

Bryan Tolley

Illustrated by Frank Capon

Wayland Publishers England

Contents

Introduction

This book shows you how to make a whole range of musical instruments for yourself. It begins with a simple pair of claves, and goes on to various wind and stringed instruments, and ends with a hurdy-gurdy. Most of these are tuned so that they can be played with other musical instruments, such as guitars or the piano.

Several of the projects are based on instruments from the Middle Ages. During this time, musical instruments were made purely for the sound they gave, not for their volume or the range of notes they could produce. Most medieval instruments were straightforward in their construction. Although the instruments might seem simple today, medieval musicians were highly skilled, often on more than one type of instrument.

In recent years, people have realized the difference it makes to play early music on copies of the original instruments. A tune written in the 12th century was intended to be played on an instrument that the composer knew well, such as the fiddle or the harp, and not on an electric organ! People began to make whole families, or consorts, of different-sized instruments. This increased the range of sounds that a single instrument could make.

Consort playing was popular in Europe during the 16th century. Many strange-sounding wind instruments were developed, with even stranger names like the crumhorn and the rackett. Even Henry VIII had a crumhorn. Instruments at this time could play only either loud or soft music. They were described simply as outdoor or indoor instruments. Outdoor instruments included trumpets, shawms (a kind of loud oboe), and drums. Recorders, and most stringed instruments such as the viol and the harpsichord, were played indoors. The lute was a very popular instrument during the 16th century.

During the 17th and 18th centuries, many instruments were redesigned. This gave them more range, and made it possible for them to play both loud and soft music. Many of our modern orchestral instruments were designed and made in this period. As a result, the earlier instruments began to disappear. Folk musicians have kept many of the old instruments and styles of playing alive.

Many instruments have long and interesting histories. One of these is the hurdy-gurdy. This is not, as it is commonly thought, a type of barrel-organ, but an ingenious mechanical fiddle. It started life as a large, two-man instrument, played in church. One man would play the tune on its keys. The other would turn a wheel that rubbed on the strings to make them sound. The hurdy-gurdy was in competition with the organ as the main instrument used in churches. When it lost this contest, sometime in the 13th century, it lost favour with the church, and eventually became a beggar's instrument. By this time, it had become small enough for one man to play, and was often used by blind beggars who could not use a bow. This is how the hurdy-gurdy stayed for hundreds of years. Then, in 18th-century France, it became the fashionable instrument for the rich to play.

Even if you are not too good with your hands, you should still be able to make some of the simpler instruments in this book. The psalteries, fiddles, and hurdy-gurdies in the photographs were all made by girls aged between 12 and 14, who had no earlier woodworking experience. Take each project in easy stages, try not to rush, and you will find that making your own musical instruments is not as difficult as it might look.

Tools

As far as possible, the tools used in this book are the standard woodworking and metalworking tools that can be found in any school workshop. Many of the instruments can be built at home, because basic tools are often all that are needed. A vice is useful and so is a pillar drill to make the projects easier to construct. The wooden instruments will need at least one coat of varnish to stop them from getting dirty. For this, use a clear polyurethane varnish. To give a better finish, put it on with a wad of cloth rather than a brush. Lightly sand down your last coat of varnish with flour paper or fine wire wool, and then put on some beeswax polish to complete the finish. When glue is needed, use a white PVA adhesive.

If you cannot get some of the parts for your instruments, don't be afraid to experiment. Try using other materials, or alter the design to suit what is available. If you cannot get music wire, for example, the wire used in the school laboratory for sound experiments will do, or wire used in steel-strung guitars.

One final touch to any instrument is to put on it the maker's name. Either glue a name tag inside, or write your name on the instrument before you varnish it. Take your time and have fun.

TECHNIQUE AND PROJECT

Claves

The first 10 instruments in this book are all known as members of the percussion family. Percussion instruments are played by being struck with a stick or hand, or struck together in pairs. Claves are simply a pair of sticks that are struck against each other. They are used to add a lively rhythm to a piece of music. Instruments such as these have been used by people all over the world for thousands of years. They can be found today in the percussion sections of Latin-American dance bands.

Many different materials may be used to make claves. Each will give its own individual sound. Stone, metal, bone, and hardwood all work well, but you will find that softwoods such as pine will not ring and will sound rather dull. Try experimenting with different materials and see what sounds you can produce.

Materials, tools, and equipment
2 pieces of a hardwood, such as rosewood, 250 × 25 mm square, *or*
2 lengths of copper tubing 250 × 13 mm diameter
Vice, rasp, or file
Three grades of glass paper: coarse, medium, and fine (flour)
Small block of wood to wrap glass paper round

Method Claves seem to work best if they are round in section, so to make the wooden set you will have to round off all the corners of the blocks. When you do this, work with one block at a

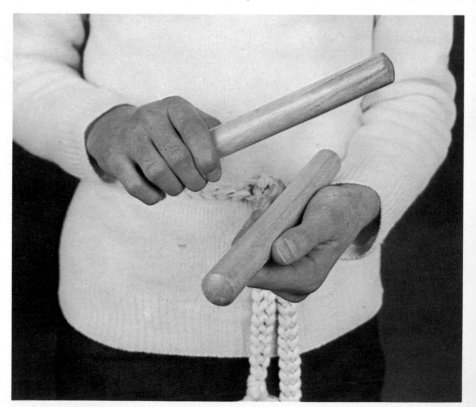

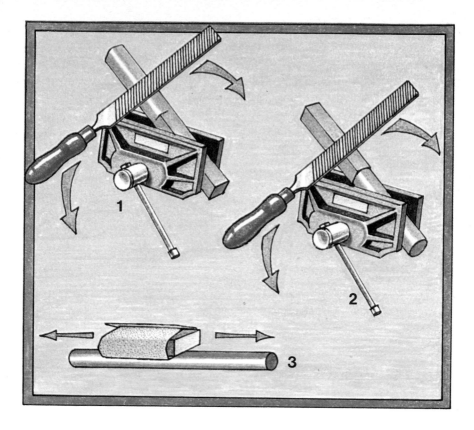

time, and use a strong woodworker's vice. Hold about half the block in the vice. Set it so that it is at a comfortable angle for you to use the rasp. Hold the handle of the rasp firmly with one hand, guiding its other end with your free hand. If your are right-handed, you will find it easier to hold the handle in your right hand. Cut away one edge at a time, pushing the rasp round the corner as you work. This will ensure a rounded edge and a smoother pair of claves **(1)**. When you have finished the exposed part of the block, turn it round in the vice, and complete the other edges. Repeat the procedure for the other block **(2)**.

Once you feel the blocks are rounded off enough, you can start to sand them down to remove any rough spots or scratches. Remember that it is easier to get rid of any big bumps with the rasp. It takes a long time with glass paper. Start by using coarse glass paper to rub along the length of the claves **(3)**. As the wood gets smoother, use a finer grade of glass paper. Finish them off with either very fine glass paper (flour paper), or with very fine wire wool. It will not be necessary to varnish your claves, but a good coating of beeswax polish helps to protect the wood and keep it looking nice.

The claves can also be made from tubing, such as the copper tubing used by plumbers when installing or repairing central heating systems. If you can get some of this, or something similar, it is an easy step to produce some excellent claves. All you have to do is saw the tubing into two pieces the same length, and remove all the sharp edges with a file. Clean them up with some fine wire wool. Finally polish them with metal polish to produce an impressive-looking pair of claves.

Bottle chimes

Chimes are also percussion instruments, but, unlike the claves, they are tuned. In other words, when each bottle is struck it will produce a different note, so that tunes as well as rhythms can be played. We can now divide the percussion family into instruments which are tuned, such as the xylophone, and those which are untuned, like the claves. Usually instruments that are used to keep time, like drums and claves, are kept untuned so they will not sound wrong when the rest of the band is playing.

In 1949, in Indo-China, a set of prehistoric stone chimes was discovered. These are probably the oldest surviving tuned percussion instruments in the world today.

The idea of the bottle chime is very simple. If the bottle is hit when empty it will give a high note. This note will sound lower as water is added to the bottle, since the water slows down the vibrations of the glass. By carefully adjusting the amount of water in each bottle a simple scale of notes can be made, allowing the chimes to be played in tune with other instruments. Al-

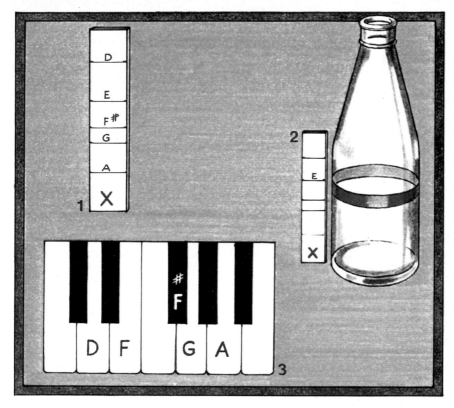

though the basic idea is simple it can be used to produce a very elaborate instrument. Indian musicians have used rows of different-sized rice bowls filled and tuned with water to produce a delicate-sounding xylophone. It is possible to play music that is beautiful and expressive on such instruments.

Materials, tools, and equipment
Five 1-pint glass bottles
A strip of stiff cardboard
Coloured adhesive tape
2 pieces of 13 mm dowel 250 mm long
Sand paper

Method   It is possible to produce the first notes of the scale of D major using five one-pint bottles. Make a ruler out of the strip of card, and use it to measure the water levels in the bottles. Mark one end of the card with a coloured cross. Then measure accurately 27 mm from this end, and draw a line across the card. Label this line A. From

the same end measure 54 mm, draw another line and label this G. Repeat this procedure at 64 mm (F sharp), 83 mm (E), and at 116 mm (D). You should now have a ruler like that shown in the diagram **(1)**. This is now used as a guide to stick rings of tape around the bottles, so the top of the tape is level with the mark on the ruler **(2)**. Fill the bottles carefully with water up to the top of the tape, and your chimes are ready to play.

It helps if you can check your tuning with a piano, because not all bottles give the same sound to start with. The notes you need can be found in the middle of a piano keyboard by comparing the diagram **(3)** with the layout of the black and white keys.

Smooth off any rough edges on the dowel with sand paper, and use these as beaters for your chimes. Metal or plastic knitting needles also make good beaters and give a different sort of sound.

11

Medieval triangle

The triangle is a simple but effective instrument with its own special sound. Modern orchestras use triangles in their percussion sections because their clear ringing notes can be heard above the other instruments.

The triangle probably appeared sometime during the 13th century when illustrated manuscripts showed it being played. At this time the triangle was fitted with rings that jingled as it was played. Sometimes medieval triangles even had four sides! Four-sided triangles lasted until the 16th century. Triangles with rings only became rare early in the 19th century. The medieval triangle with rings looks similar to an ancient type of rattle known as the sistrum. Like the sistrum the triangle can also be shaken to make a sound.

Materials, tools, and equipment
8 mm diameter steel bar
3 or 4 metal curtain or key rings
A piece of strong twine
Hammer, centre-punch, file, hacksaw
2 mm drill

Method   Nearly all triangles and their beaters are made of steel. Scientists have analysed the type of steel used in the Middle Ages, and found it is similar to what we now know as silver steel. You can use silver steel for your triangle, but it will be more expensive. Ordinary steel will work almost as well.

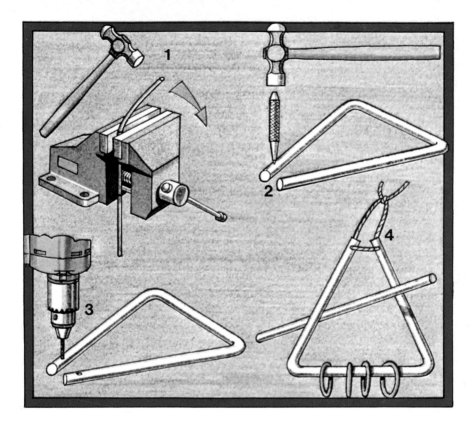

Begin by sawing off 325 mm of steel bar. Remove the rough edges with a file. Make a mark 108 mm in from each end of the bar. This is where the bar is to be bent. Place the bar in a vice, with one mark level with the top of the vice jaws. Using the hammer bend the bar down as far as you can **(1)**. Remove the bar from the vice, and check on the angle you have made. It should be about 60 degrees. If not, return it to the vice, and bend it again until it is correct. The other side of the triangle is bent in the same way, and left so there is a small gap between the two ends of the bar.

With the centre-punch and the hammer, make two small dots 5 mm away from each end of the triangle **(2)**. With the 2 mm drill, carefully drill right through the bar where the dots have been placed. These holes are for the twine **(3)**.

If you want a triangle with rings, these can now be put on the instrument. Use three or four brass curtain rings, or some metal key rings, or washers. If these are not available it is a simple matter to cut the heads and points off some 4″ nails, and using the vice and hammer bend these into loops. Thread a piece of twine through both holes in the triangle, and tie the ends together to make a loop. This will give you something to hold the instrument with, and it also stops the rings from falling off.

Finally saw off about 200 mm of steel bar and file off all the rough edges to make your beater **(4)**. Try experimenting with different types of rings and jingles to see what sounds you can make. If you leave all the rings off, the triangle will make a familiar ring, if it is suspended properly. Should the triangle buzz or rattle without any rings on it, check that there is still a gap at the top of the instrument.

Nail chimes

One instrument that is simple to make and has a pleasant, delicate sound is the nail chime. This consists of a series of large nails hung by a thread from a frame. The nails are sawn to different lengths so that when they are struck they sound at different pitches. Like the bottle chimes, the nail chimes belong to the tuned section of the percussion family.

For these chimes to work well they must be hung using the lightest thread.

String or wire will deaden the sound by not letting the nails vibrate freely. Although these chimes are not loud they have a lovely sweet ring, and are very cheap to make.

Nails have been used for other instruments too. In the 18th century a musician invented the nail fiddle. This had a circular soundbox with nails of different lengths sticking up from it. The nail fiddle was held in one hand, and played with a violin bow held in the other. It was said to have a very beautiful sound.

Materials, tools, and equipment
Five 6″ round nails
Four 4″ round nails
900 mm length of 13 mm dowel
10 mm plywood, glue
Button thread, hacksaw, file, drill

Method Start your chimes by making the frame to support the nails. This is

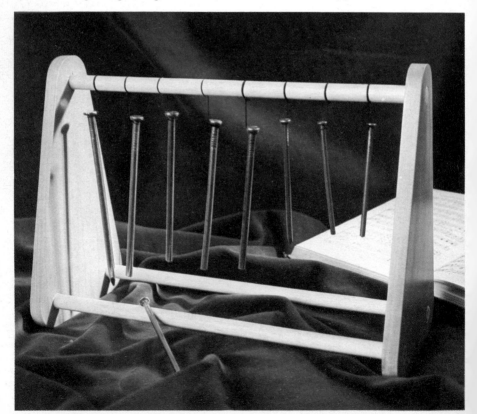

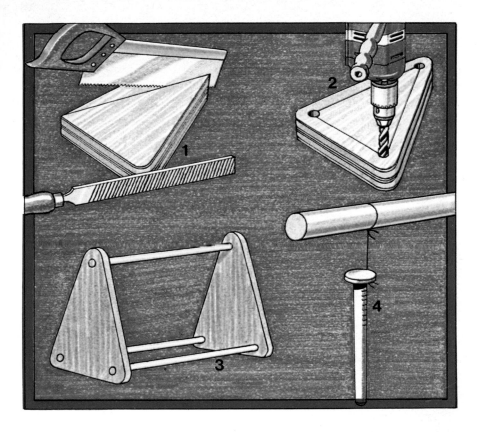

made of two plywood sides, and three lengths of dowel to hold it all together. Cut two rectangles of plywood 225 by 150 mm. Place one piece exactly on top of the other. Mark the centre of one of the short edges. Draw a triangle from this point to the two opposite corners of the sides. Keeping the two pieces of wood together, saw them carefully to shape, and take off the sharp corners with a file **(1)**. With the two sides still together, draw another triangle on the top one 15 mm in from the edge all round. At each corner of this triangle drill a 12 mm hole right through both pieces of wood **(2)**. Now saw the dowel into three 300 mm lengths. Glue the ends of these into the holes in the plywood sides to complete the frame **(3)**.

An ordinary 6" round nail produces the note D when it is struck, while a 4" round nail gives the note B. This is very useful since it means that by using five 6" nails, and three 4" nails, a complete scale of D major can be made. This will be in tune with the bottle chimes. If a nail is sawn off short, it will sound at a higher note. This is how you get the other notes for the scale. Take four of the 6" nails. Saw the pointed end off one to leave it at exactly 140 mm long. Saw the remaining three nails accurately to 130 mm, 126 mm, and 120 mm long. Remove all the sharp edges carefully with a file. Now take two of the 4" nails and saw them in the same way to 89 mm, and 86 mm long.

To hang the nails, tie a length of thread around the head of the nail, and then over the top bar of the frame **(4)**. Finally tie all the other nails up in order of length, with the whole 6" nail at one end, and the shortest 4" nail at the other. The remaining 4" nail is the beater for your chimes.

Rommelpot

The rommelpot is a traditional Flemish folk instrument that makes a roaring noise like the sound of thunder. It is a type of friction drum. The drum skin is set vibrating by a hand being rubbed along a stick or cord attached to the skin. The word 'rommelen' means to do something quickly but awkwardly, so as not to show what you are doing. Another meaning of the word is 'to produce a dull noise'.

Rommelpots can be made from almost any container; earthenware flowerpots are ideal. Usually the rommelpot is a small instrument. The friction drum is not a solo instrument, but is used to accompany singing.

In Belgium it is played with the 'Sterre-Liederen'. This is a ritual where three musicians wander around the village streets between Christmas and Epiphany, representing the three wise kings from the east. The leader sings, and carries a star tied to a pole; he is followed by a lantern bearer, and finally a rommelpot player. Each person is made up with soot, pig's blood, and flour. These stand for the symbolic colours: black for death, red for gifts, and white for life. Their songs ask for money, not for themselves, but for the rommelpot. With such a strange name

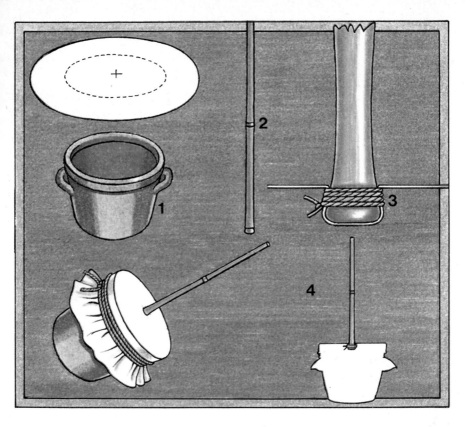

nd voice, it is not surprising that the
nstrument has a personality!

Materials, tools, and equipment
small earthenware pot or bowl
a sheet of vellum or strong polythene
thin rope
cane, twine, and a pair of scissors

Method Choose a suitable container
for your rommelpot, such as a flower-
pot, or a bowl with a lip around its edge.
Traditionally the skin on the top of the
pot should be made from a pig's blad-
der. Unless you can obtain one, use
other drum or banjo vellum from a
music shop, or some strong polythene
sheet. Cut the material into a circle
larger than the top of the pot so that it
can overhang below the lip on the rim
of the pot **(1)**. Choose a piece of
smooth, thin cane, with a knot at one
end, and at least 250 mm long **(2)**. Mark
the centre of the skin where the stick is

to fit. If you are using vellum, soak it in
cold water for about fifteen minutes to
soften it ready for working. Gently
stretch out the centre of the skin with
the end of the stick, and then tightly
bind the stick in place with the twine
(3). While the vellum is still wet, stretch
it over the pot, and lash it on firmly with
the rope **(4)**. As it dries out the skin will
shrink and pull taut. If you use natural
rope, use it wet, as this also shrinks and
pulls tight as it dries. Do the same as
above for the plastic-covered version,
without the soaking process.

To play the rommelpot, moisten your
right hand, and hold the pot against
your chest with your left hand. Pull the
cane with your wet hand, and as it
begins to dry out the pot will start to
speak. Be prepared for some strange
noises!

Sometimes these instruments are
partly filled with some dried peas, or
grit, to add to the sound.

17

Sistrum

The sistrum is an early percussion instrument belonging to the rattle family. It has been found all over the world, in ancient Egypt, Rome, West Africa, Malaya, and even amongst North American Indians.

Rattles are said to have magical properties, and are often found as part of a witch doctor's equipment. A sistrum is a special type of rattle consisting of a frame with jingles on it. An ancient Egyptian sistrum was a metal frame with bars and a handle. The jingles were on the bars of this frame. This sistrum had to be shaken about like a baby's rattle to be sounded.

The type of sistrum described for you to make is based on a simple Belgian folk instrument. Although it was once a popular instrument, this form of sistrum (or Rammelaar as it is known in Belgium) seems to have become rare early this century. It was used especially to accompany songs o Christmas, and Epiphany, but o course it has a great many other uses This sistrum is normally played by holding it in one hand and beating it against the opposite hand or forearm.

Materials, tools, and equipment
Some pine 350 × 50 × 10 mm
3 nails or screws, some sheet metal
Tin snips, drill, spokeshave, rasp
Centre-punch, glass paper

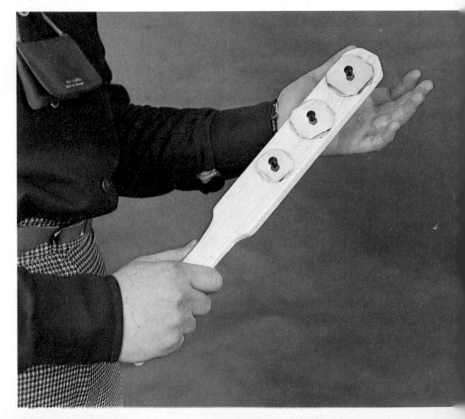

Method Start by marking the shape of the sistrum on the piece of pine. The corners are all rounded off, and one end is shaped for a handle. The actual shape of the sistrum does not really matter as the sizes are not very important. Just try to get a shape like that in the diagram **(1)**. Shape the corners first with a saw, round them off with the rasp, and finally sand them smooth. The handle can be shaped using the spokeshave, and then sanded smooth.

For the jingles any odd scraps of metal will do. Copper was often used, but brass or steel will do just as well. Avoid using tinplate as this is too thin, and will not work very well. Cut the metal into nine squares about 35 mm across and snip off all the sharp corners. Decide whether you are using screws or nails to hold the jingles. If you want to use nails make sure they have large heads or else the jingles will come off. Mark the centres of the squares and make a dot with a centre-punch. Drill a hole in each square, larger than the size of the screw or nail **(2)**. Screw or nail loosely three sets of three jingles onto the wooden handle and your Belgian sistrum is complete **(3)**.

Jingle stick Another simple rattle is the jingle stick. This can easily be made from a broomstick, some nails, and several tops from beer or cola bottles. After removing the inserts, drill a hole through the centre of each bottle top. Fit two tops back to back on a nail, and then drive this into the side of the broomstick near one end **(4)**. If you have enough bottle tops and nails to cover the whole of one end of the broomstick, you will get a really effective jingle stick. This instrument is often painted in bright colours, and is sounded by being pounded up and down on the ground.

Tubular bells

Most orchestras these days have their own set of tubular bells. Although they are called bells they look nothing like those you would expect to see in a church tower. Tubular bells are simply tubes of metal sounded by being struck at the top with a leather-covered hammer. One famous piece of music, Tchaikovsky's 1812 Overture, uses tubular bells to imitate church bells pealing in victory after battle.

The bells that you can make are in the musical scale or key of C major. This is a very common key that will allow you to play tunes with other instruments. Copper tubing is used to make the bells. It is generally used for water pipes, and can be bought from your local plumber or hardware store. Although the construction is very similar to the nail chimes, the finished instrument is larger, louder, and has a completely different sound. They really do sound like bells.

Materials, tools, and equipment
12 mm plywood, 19 mm dowel
12 mm copper tubing
Button thread, hacksaw, file, drill
6" nail, glue, centre-punch

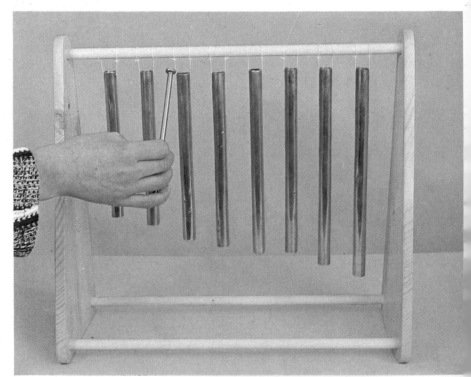

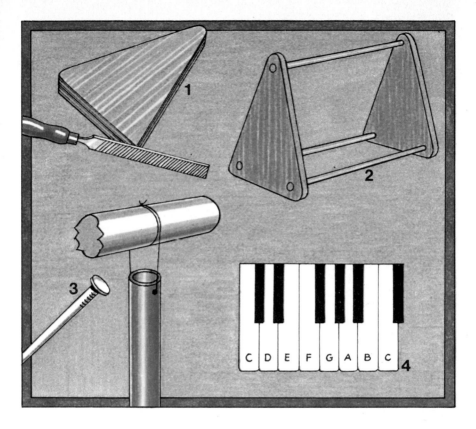

Method Begin by making the frame. This is basically the same as the nail chime frame, but it is larger and stronger. Saw two rectangles of 12 mm plywood, 380 × 200 mm and place one piece on top of the other. Mark a triangle on the top one going from one corner to the centre of a short edge, and down again to the opposite corner. Keeping both pieces of wood together, saw them into a triangle, and saw off the sharp corners **(1)**. Draw a triangle 25 mm in from the edge of the pieces of wood, and with both pieces still together drill a 19 mm hole at each corner of this triangle. Next cut the dowel into three 400 mm lengths. Glue the ends of these into the holes in the sides to complete the frame **(2)**.

The bells are all made from different lengths of 12 mm diameter copper tubing. You will need eight bells. For these, saw off eight lengths of tubing to the following sizes: 252 mm, 238 mm,

221 mm, 213 mm, 209 mm, 201 mm, 185 mm, 175 mm. When you are sawing the tubes hold them gently in a vice, being careful not to squash them. At 6 mm from one end of each tube make a dot with a centre-punch and drill right through the tube with a 2 mm drill. Remove all sharp edges with a file. Pass some thread through the holes on the longest tube, and tie this to the top bar of the frame **(3)**. Then hang up the other tubes in order of size, from one end of the frame to the other.

A hammer tor the bells is made from a 6″ nail with the point filed off. Use the head of the nail to strike the bells. Do this near the top of the tubes, or else you will find they swing about a lot.

Your tubular bells are now complete and should be in tune with a scale of C major on the piano **(4)**. Eight bells give you an 'octave' – this means that the top note has the same name as the bottom note but sounds higher.

Sansa

The sansa is a tuned percussion instrument consisting of a box fitted with metal rods that are plucked to make it sound. Sometimes known as a finger piano, the sansa is a very old instrument, first discovered by travellers in Africa in 1586.

The instrument has been fitted to the top of a box, which makes the vibrating rods sound louder. This is called a soundbox, and is often used for stringed instruments where the sound of the strings needs to be made louder. On the soundbox the sansa has several metal rods or tongues held in between wooden bridges. The tongues are usually made of iron or steel, beaten out until it is flat and springy. In some areas of Africa the sansa is fitted with thin strips of bamboo.

Materials, tools, and equipment
3 mm plywood 180 × 125 mm
60 cm of pine 12 × 35 mm
375 mm of triangular moulding
Two 1½" No. 6 woodscrews, 1" panel
　pins
16-gauge piano wire, glue

Method　To start the sansa it is necessary to make the soundbox. First the wood has to be cut to size. Start with the sides of the box. Cut two pieces of pine 180 mm and two pieces 100 mm long. Make a frame out of these by join-

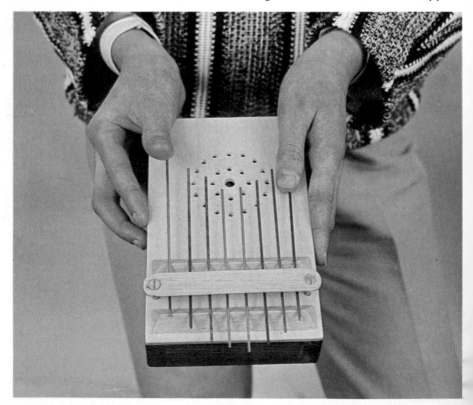

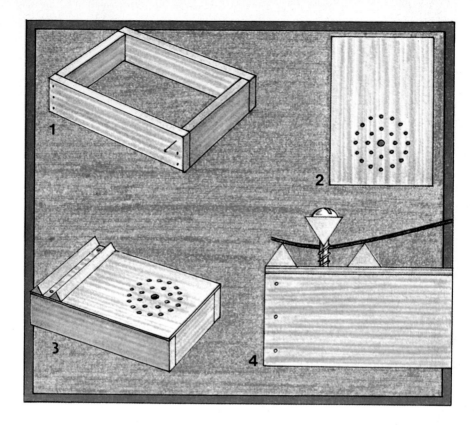

ing the ends of the shorter pieces of wood to the sides of the ends of the longer pieces of wood. When you are sure it is correct, apply the glue, and pin it together using the panel pins. Leave it to dry **(1)**.

Lay the frame on the plywood and mark around the edge of it on the plywood. Remove the frame, and saw the plywood to the correct size. Doing it this way should ensure a good fit. The plywood is the top of the soundbox and is known as the soundboard. The soundboard usually has a hole in it – like the hole in the soundboard of a guitar. This allows the sound to come out of the box. A simple and decorative way of doing this is to use a compass, mark out a simple pattern, and then drill holes at the points on the pattern **(2)**. This type of soundhole is known as a rose, and was always used on lutes and similar stringed instruments. Make the centre of your rose design in the

middle of the soundboard, and 63 mm up from the bottom edge. Glue the soundboard onto the frame.

Saw off three 125 mm lengths of the moulding for the bridges. Glue two of these on the soundboard at the opposite end from the rose **(3)**. Drill two holes in the third bridge 6 mm in from each end. These holes should be the right size for the screws. Screw the bridge down between the two bridges glued to the soundboard. Do not screw it right down, but leave a gap for the rods.

Piano wire is a good springy wire that can be bought at model shops. Cut eight 150 mm lengths and fit these in between the bridges. Then tighten the screws until all the rods are secure **(4)**. To tune the sansa, the wire is pulled out to lower the note, or pushed in to raise the note. Hold the sansa with both hands and pluck the wire with your thumbs.

Drumsticks

If you have a drum or intend to make a drum you will need some drumsticks. There are many different types of stick which can be used. Each one makes a different sound when it strikes the drum. Perhaps the most usual is the one shaped like a club, with a body that thins down and ends in a round knob. This sort of drumstick can be made in various thicknesses, depending upon whether you want to have a solid beat or a light and decorative rhythm. The shape of the drumstick is designed so that it will not tear the drum-skin. As long as the sharp edges are taken off, any wooden rod may be used as a drumstick.

Some drumsticks are made with large soft ends on them. These give the drum a full booming sound, as opposed to the crisp sound from the other types of drumstick.

Drumsticks can also be used for other instruments. For example, the psaltery that is described later in the book can also be beaten with sticks instead of being plucked. When played this way the instrument is known as a dulcimer, and is played in many parts of the world. Sticks for the psaltery, or rather dulcimer, should be soft at the end so that they make a gentle and not a harsh sound when the string is struck.

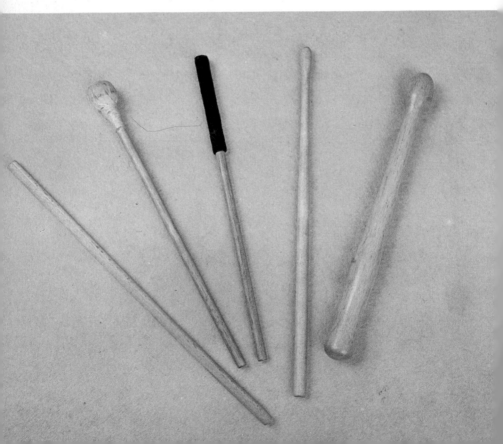

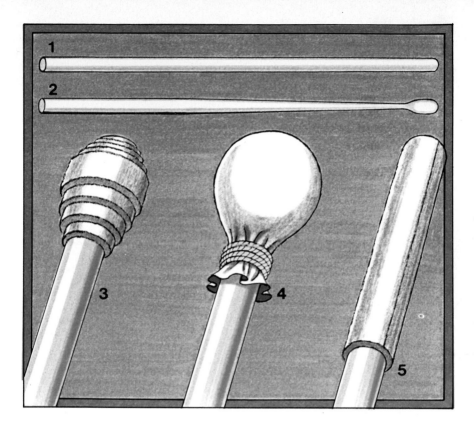

Materials, tools, and equipment
Wooden dowel in various sizes
Felt, cotton cloth, string, glue,
   sandpaper, knife, saw

Method The easiest sticks to make are those made from wooden rod or dowel. Use a piece of 10 mm diameter dowel. Saw it to about 300 mm length. To finish the stick, smooth off the rough edges with sandpaper **(1)**.

The shaped sticks are a bit more difficult. Begin by sawing the dowel to the same length as before. Sand off the rough edges. Using a sharp knife, carefully shape the body of the drumstick so that it tapers towards one end. Leave enough wood to shape the tip **(2)**.

Sand the whole stick down, removing the sharp edges.

To make a light drumstick, use a piece of 8 mm dowel, and for a heavy drumstick use up to 25 mm dowel.

Large wooden knitting needles can be used as an alternative.

To make drumsticks with large soft ends, start with 300 mm lengths of 8 mm dowel that has had the sharp edges removed. Wrap and glue a 25 mm wide strip of felt around one end. Glue a narrower strip of felt on top, and add a narrower one still **(3)**. When the lump of felt looks large enough (about 25 mm across) cover it with a piece of cotton cloth and tie this on tight with string **(4)**. A drop of glue on the string will stop it coming untied.

To make the drumstick, or rather the beater, for a dulcimer start off with lengths of 6 mm dowel. On one end wrap a strip of felt around the dowel and glue in place **(5)**. Make another the same.

Tabor

The tabor is a common style of drum found in many different parts of the world. It has a cylindrical body or shell and a drum-skin on both ends. Tabors can come in many shapes and sizes. English folk music is generally played using a shallow tabor like a tambourine.

There is a special kind of flute known as the 'tabor pipe'. This flute has only three finger holes and is played in one hand leaving the other hand free to beat time on the tabor. Although it only has three holes, it is possible to play a full scale on the instrument.

The drum described here uses a biscuit tin for the shell. Shells are usually made from wood. This design uses a round tin as it is difficult to bend wood into a tube. The tin can be painted, and the fact that it is metal will make very little difference to the sound. This drum is not a toy but a proper musical instrument that needs looking after.

Materials, tools, and equipment
Round cake tin, biscuit tin, or similar container
Tin opener, file, paint
6 mm Terylene pre-stretched rope, cord, two squares of vellum.
Scissors, leather punch, large needle
Strip of leather 25 mm wide.

Method for making the shell To make the drum shell remove the bottom of your tin with a tin opener **(1)**.

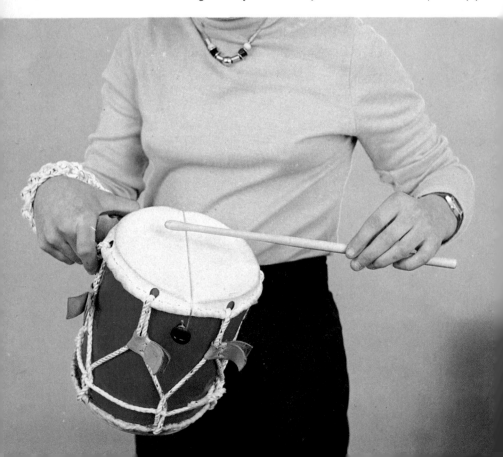

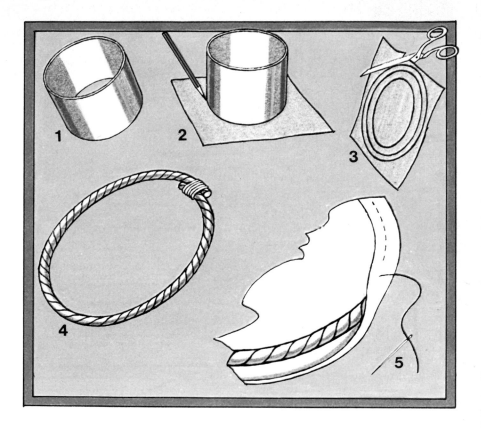

Remove any sharp edges around the top and bottom edges of the shell with a file. These sharp edges can give nasty cuts.

Now you can paint your shell. Gloss paint is best. Use bright colours. The size of your tabor depends upon the size of your shell. A shallow drum will give a crisp note whilst a deep drum will give a booming note.

The drum heads The skins on a drum are known as the heads. To make the heads for your tabor, place your shell on a piece of vellum and draw a line round it **(2)**. Sheets of vellum for drums and banjos can be bought at music shops. Make sure you know how big you need your pieces before you go to buy them. Remove the shell and draw another circle 25 mm out from the first,

and then another 20 mm further out still. Cut around the largest circle **(3)**. Soak the vellum in some water to soften it.

Take the rope and cut off enough to go round the shell once, with a 30 mm overlap. With some fine cord firmly lash the last 25 mm of the rope together to form a strong ring **(4)**. This ring should fit loosely round the shell.

The rope ring has to be sewn onto the vellum. Fold the vellum over on the larger circle and sew it up with the rope inside **(5)**. Use cord, a large needle, and a good thimble as vellum is difficult to sew. Try to get all the stitches about 5 mm long. Don't worry if it looks puckered up, it will stretch into shape later on. If it begins to get stiff, just soak the head in water for ten minutes and it will soften up again.

Tabor

fitting the heads

tensioning the drum

Fitting the heads Before the heads can be fitted on the shell they have to be pierced with holes to take the tensioning ropes. These holes are made with a leather punch. Place them as close to the line of sewing as you can get them. The number you make depends upon the size of your drum. Space them out between 50 mm and 60 mm apart all around the edge of the head. Make sure that they are equally spaced, and that the holes are large enough to take the rope (1). You will probably find that between six and

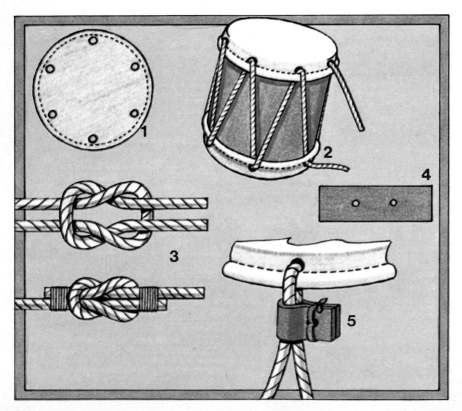

eight holes will do. Now soak the heads in water to make them soft again.

Place the softened heads on the ends of the shell. Using a long piece of rope begin to lace up the heads. Line up the heads so that the holes in the top one are in between the holes in the bottom one. Pass the rope alternately through the two heads until you have been once round the drum (2). Pull the slack out of the rope and make sure that the heads are evenly seated before you tie the ends of the rope together. Use a reef knot for this, and to make it neater lash the loose ends to the rope with some cord (3).

Tensioning the drum As the heads dry out they will shrink slightly and tighten up. To get a really good tension in the heads a second system is used. 'Buffs' or 'tug ears' are leather loops that are fitted around pairs of ropes lacing the heads together. Moving the buffs up the ropes pulls the ropes together, and in turn causes the head to be stretched. This system allows the tension to be taken off the drum when it is not in use.

To make the buffs, use a strip of leather 25 mm wide. Cut this into 75 mm lengths. You need as many lengths as you have holes in one head on your tabor.

Now make two 5 mm holes in each buff with the leather punch. These should be 25 mm apart and in the centre of the strip of leather (4). Cut some 6 mm strips of scrap vellum and soak them to make them soft. Fit the buff around two pieces of rope near to where they pass through a hole in the head. Fold the ends together. Then thread the strip of soft vellum through the holes in the buff, around the bottom, back through the hole and tie the ends in a reef knot on top (5). As the vellum dries out it will pull the knot tight and make the buff very strong.

Playing To tension the drum, simply slide the buffs along the ropes. Do this evenly all round the drum or it will sound wrong. You will need some way of holding the drum whilst you play it. One way is to hold the tensioning ropes, another to thread a belt through the ropes, and strap the tabor around your waist. A third method is to make a wrist strap from a strip of leather or some rope and fit this to the tensioning ropes. The tabor in the photograph has a wrist strap made of plaited rope and this works well and also looks good. Drums can be made to look very attractive with bright coloured paint and decorative ropework, but mainly they make a good noise.

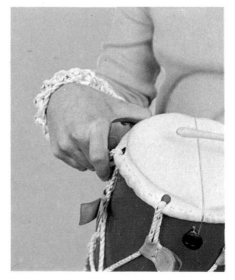

Kazoo

The kazoo is a very simple instrument that is great fun to play. You don't need any special musical knowledge to get your favourite tunes out of a kazoo. You simply sing through it. As your voice goes through the instrument it makes a thin membrane of tissue paper vibrate. This in turn amplifies and distorts the voice, so that it doesn't sound a bit human. You can of course play any tune you can sing.

A kazoo is really a sophisticated version of the comb and paper. Many bands use them for special effects, and some folk guitarists will sing through a kazoo and accompany themselves on the guitar.

You can make a kazoo from more or less anything. A cardboard tube, a piece of plastic, or metal pipe will all work equally well. Wood has been used for the instrument described below, but any tube with a membrane stuck across a hole in it will work as a kazoo.

Materials, tools, and equipment
6 mm hardwood 375 x 36 mm
Tissue paper, glue, pencil, ruler
Saw, file, sandpaper, varnish

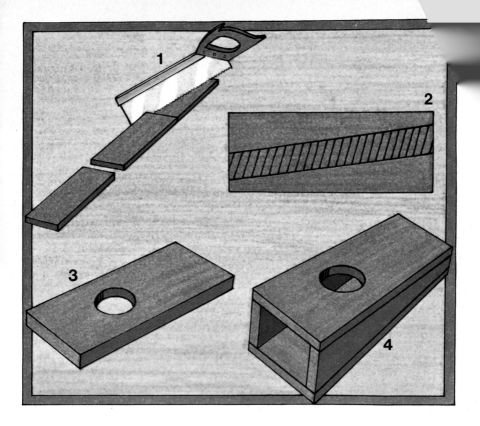

Method Divide, and saw the piece of wood into three pieces each 125 mm long **(1)**. Mark one piece for the top of the kazoo and one piece for the underside. The other piece is sawn up to form the sides.

On this kazoo the sides taper from 20 mm to 6 mm. Mark these shapes on the piece of wood and saw them out **(2)**.

Cut a hole in the top of the instrument. This is best done by first drawing out a circle 22 mm in diameter. Drill a 6 mm hole inside the circle. A coping saw can now be put in and used to saw out the circle. Another method is to drill a ring of holes inside the circle and then push out the circle. Finish off the edges of the hole with a round file and some sandpaper **(3)**.

Glue all the pieces of wood together at the same time, using a clamp or some sticky tape to hold them in place while the glue dries. Once the glue is properly hard you can use a file to get rid of all the sharp and rough edges **(4)**. Use sandpaper to get the instrument as smooth as you can. A coat or two of varnish will keep it looking nice and will stop the wood from absorbing moisture from your mouth.

To make the kazoo work, a piece of tissue paper is stuck right over the hole in the top. Try to use the hard tissue that is used for wrapping and packaging. Model aircraft tissue is too soft for this job.

Playing To play the kazoo, put the large end to your lips with the tissue membrane on the top. Try singing or humming a note through it so that you can get an idea of what kind of sound works best. Usually a cross between singing and humming seems to produce the best noise. Once you have found out what to do the kazoo will play any tune you know.

31

Panpipes

Pan was an ancient Greek god who was half-man half-goat. He did not stay with the other gods on Mount Olympus, but lived as a herdsman with the mortals in southern Greece. At night he joined in the revels of the nymphs of the woods and the hills. At these times a certain wildness would overcome him.

Pan wooed many of the nymphs. Among them was Syrinx, who fled in horror to the banks of the River Ladon and turned into a reed to escape from him. Pan cut a number of the reeds in an attempt to find her. From these he made the pipes by which he is known today.

The syrinx or panpipes have been played since the time of the ancient Greeks and have been found all over the world from Germany to South America. Although rather difficult to play, they sound really beautiful and are well worth the effort taken to learn and practise.

Materials, tools, and equipment
Bamboo cane about 12 mm diameter
Two thin strips of wood, cord, a
    candle, a piece of thin dowel, fine
    saw, sandpaper

Method This is a set of nine pipes giving the instrument a scale of G major plus a top A. You will need to tune each

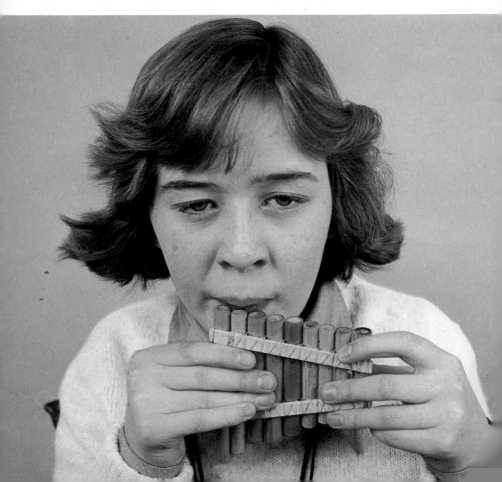

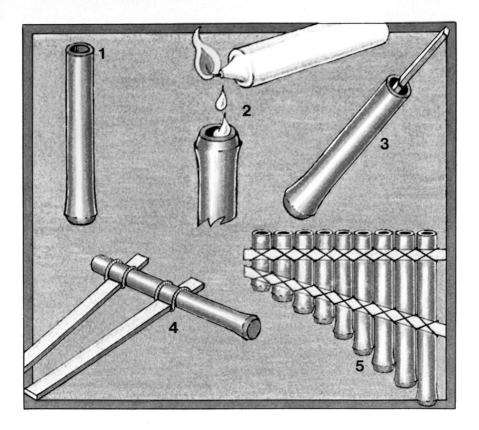

pipe as you make it. Do not rush it because the tuning is important.

Start with the longest pipe and saw it off to 130 mm. Make sure there is a knot in the bamboo right at one end of your pipe (1). A knot is where there is a lump in the cane and at this point the hole down the centre is blocked. You need a length of tube that is blocked at one end. If there is no knot, seal it with a couple of drops of wax from a candle (2). Remove any pith or fur from inside the tube with a piece of rolled-up sand-paper.

Mark a length 107 mm down on a piece of dowel. Use this as a gauge (3). Carefully saw the tube down until the length from the top edge to the top of the knot on the inside of the tube is 107 mm. When the tube is the right length try blowing across it. It should sound the note G. Check this with a piano or a recorder. If your pipe sounds too low (flat), saw some more off and

try again. If your pipe sounds too high (sharp), the best thing is to use it for the next pipe up and start to make the first pipe again.

When one pipe is finished make eight others using the same method and the following inside lengths; 94 mm, 82 mm, 77 mm, 69 mm, 61 mm, 56 mm, 49 mm, 44 mm.

Take two thin strips of wood about 130 mm long. Tie each pipe to the strips of wood with cord or thin string. If you are not good at making knots, a drop of glue might help (4). Tie the pipes side by side so that they are arranged in order of size and their tops are straight and level (5). Trim off the ends of the wooden strips and your pipes are complete.

When playing the pipes keep the wooden strips in front and blow a thin stream of air across the hole, aiming at the back edge. It will take a lot of prac-tising to play well.

Transverse flute

The flute is usually known as one of the principal instruments of the woodwind family. It has a strong but sweet tone that can easily rise above the other instruments of the orchestra. If you have ever seen a concert flute you will probably have noticed how complicated it looks with all its keys and mechanisms. Four hundred years ago the flute was a wooden tube with six finger holes, yet it could still produce a good sound and had a large range of notes.

Going even farther back in history, tens of thousands of years, there is evidence that primitive flutes were being played. These were made of bone, reed or from cane and usually had no finger holes. Different notes (harmonics) were obtained by blowing harder. In these early times the sounds the flutes made were regarded as magic. The tribal medicine man would use a flute to talk to the spirits, to cure sickness, to stop rain and in all sorts of rituals.

The flute described for you to make is made of copper water pipe. Using this material means the flute is easy to make and also very strong. It is tuned to a scale of G major.

Materials, tools, and equipment
Copper tubing 22 mm diameter,
    420 mm long
A cork to fit the tube
7, 8, 9, and 10 mm drills
Ruler, small round file, emery cloth
Hacksaw, metal polish

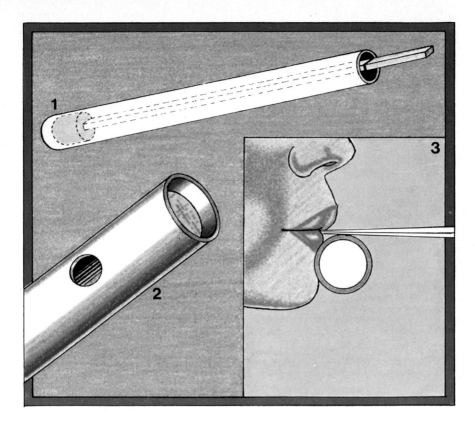

Method for making the body All the work on a wind instrument has to be very accurate as it usually affects the tuning. Once the tuning is out the instrument is of little use. Take your time making the flute. Although there is not a lot to it, it does need to be done carefully.

Saw off the length of tubing for the body and clean up the sharp edges at the ends with the round file and some emery cloth. Emery cloth is a kind of sandpaper for metal. If you can't get any, fine sandpaper will do, but it will wear out quickly.

Check that the cork you have fits nicely in the tube and will not let any air leak past. Measure 387 mm from one end of a scrap strip of wood, and draw a line. Use this wood as a gauge inside the flute. Push the cork in so that its end is 387 mm from the end of the flute **(1)**. Once the cork is set, don't move it. Make a note of which end you meas-

ured from as this is where all the other sizes will be taken from.

The embouchure The embouchure is a special name given to the mouth hole in a flute. In this design the embouchure is a hole drilled exactly 374 mm from the end of the flute and 10 mm in diameter **(2)**. Once the hole is made, get rid of any sharp pieces of copper sticking up (burrs). Don't round off the edges to the hole, these should remain sharp.

It should now be possible to get the first notes out of your flute. Put it to your chin below your lips and blow gently across the embouchure **(3)**. Blow in a thin stream so that the air just touches the back of the hole, and gradually adjust your blowing until the flute speaks clearly. If all has gone well this note should be a G. Try blowing harder and see how many other notes or rather harmonics you can get.

35

Transverse

flute

tuning

playing

Tuning the flute To tune the flute to play more than just the harmonics, finger holes are needed. Six are usually enough. These have to be placed in the proper position in line with the embouchure and made to the right size.

Measure 72 mm from the end of the flute. Drill a hole 8 mm in diameter. To make sure the drill doesn't slip, it is a

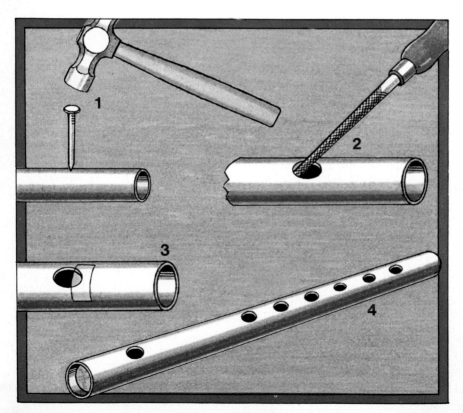

good idea to make a small dot in the metal first. This can either be done with a tool called a centre-punch or a hammer and nail. Put the nail on the tube as if you were going to hammer it in, instead give one gentle tap to dot the metal (1). Start to drill with the drill in the dot and your work will be more accurate.

This hole will be a bit too small and will give the note A a bit lower (flat) than it should be. To bring it up to correct pitch (sharper), the hole has to be made slightly bigger by filing away the edges (2). Keep checking the note to make sure you haven't filed away too much. It is easy to sharpen a note, but it is also easy to go too far. If the note does become too high it can be flattened by putting sticky tape partly across the hole until it gives the right note (3).

All the time you are making the flute you must keep checking the notes against another instrument like a piano or a recorder.

The second hole B is 10 mm in diameter, the third C is 7 mm in diameter, the fourth D is 9 mm in diameter, the fifth E is 10 mm in diameter, and the sixth hole F sharp is 9 mm in diameter. These holes are at the following distances from the end of the flute; B 98 mm, C 124 mm, D 154 mm, E 184 mm, F sharp 212 mm. Drill and tune all the holes in the same way that the first hole was made. If all has gone correctly you should find that the holes are all about 1 mm in diameter larger than the original drilled holes. Polish up the flute to finish it off (4).

Playing the flute Getting a good sound out of the instrument is the hardest part and needs the most practice. Not only is the mouth hole called the embouchure, but the term is also applied to the flute player's mouth, and the shape of his lips. It is their embouchure that beginners have to develop. Try to avoid smiling when playing. This makes your lips too tense and gives a thin breathy sound.

Hold the flute to your right, with the right hand on the bottom three finger holes, and the left hand round the front of the flute and on the top three finger holes. Look at the photograph and you will see the correct position.

To play a scale take one finger off after another in order, starting nearest to the end of the flute. When you get up to F sharp, with all your fingers off, the next note G is obtained by putting all your fingers down again and blowing harder. For notes higher than this second G keep taking your fingers off in order and blowing harder.

Recorder

The recorder is a very common instrument these days. People tend to think of their use in schools and shudder at the idea. This is unfair, as the recorder was a classic member of the woodwind family long before clarinets, oboes and bassoons were invented. During Bach's time orchestras always used recorders instead of flutes because they could play louder. Today most orchestras use metal flutes to play Bach's music, but this is not how he would have heard it.

In the 16th century recorders were played in sets or consorts of different sizes. Much of the music written for them then still remains. The first recorders appeared in the 13th century. Recently one was discovered in Holland, showing us how instruments were made so long ago.

The instrument described below is not a true recorder, but a member of the recorder family known as a flageolet. Flageolets were often used in the 18th century to teach cage birds to sing tunes.

Materials, tools, and equipment
2 pieces sycamore 460 x 25 x 6 mm
2 pieces sycamore 460 x 13 x 6 mm
Block of pine 36 x 13 mm square
Glue, chisel, drills, sandpaper,
    varnish, saw, plane, file, some
    beeswax.

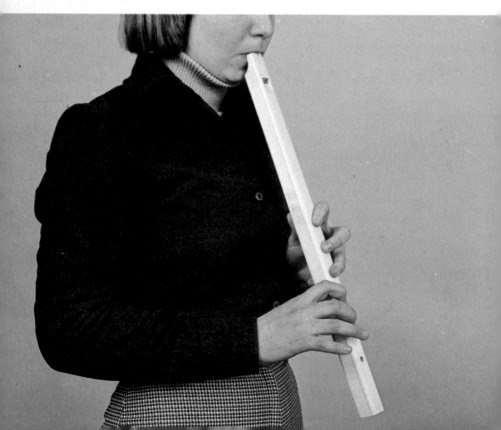

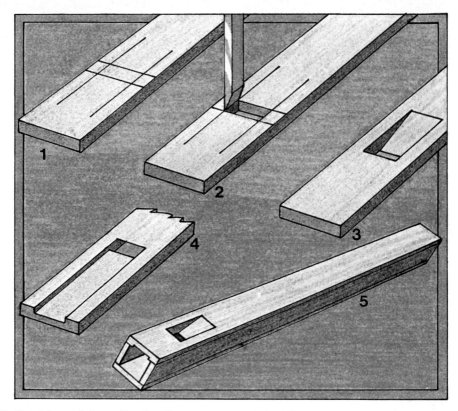

Method for voicing On the flute you make a sound by blowing air across the instrument with your lips. On the recorder this is done for you by a passage called the windway. This directs your breath onto a sharp edge that makes the instrument sound. Making the windway and cutting the sharp edge are the first, and trickiest, parts to making this recorder. If something goes wrong at this stage it is better to start again.

Take one long strip of wood 25 mm wide and draw a line across it 37 mm from the end. Follow this with another line 44 mm from the same end. Measure 7 mm in from each side of the wood and draw a line along, forming a rectangle in the centre of the wood **(1)**.

Using a 3 mm drill, carefully drill a hole inside each corner of the rectangle. Do not go outside these lines. Find a 6 mm mortise chisel that is very sharp. Chisel out all the wood from inside the rectangle, leaving the sides

straight **(2)**.

Draw another line across your strip of wood 20 mm in front of the hole. From this line chisel out the wood so that it slopes to the bottom of the hole **(3)**. When you get close to the bottom of the hole take it steady, since it is easy to chop off too much and ruin the voicing. Try to get a straight, sharp edge.

Turn the strip over and draw two more lines from the edges of the hole to the end of the strip. Very carefully chisel out a channel between these lines so that it is 1.5 mm deep at the hole end and 2 mm deep at the end of the strip **(4)**.

The Body The body of the instrument is square, so you can make it without having to use a machine called a lathe. Make the body by gluing your strips of wood together to make a tube. Hold it together with sticky tape while the glue dries **(5)**.

Recorder
fitting the block
tuning
playing

Fitting the block The pine block of wood fits tightly in the end of your recorder and acts as the bottom of the windway. It should be the right size, but if not check to see which side is too big and plane some off. Take only one or two cuts with the plane as it is easy to remove too much wood. Try to get a

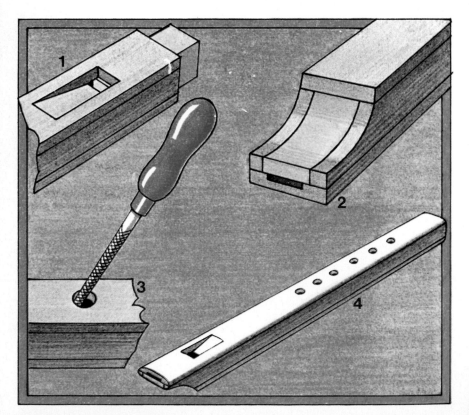

ight fit in the end of your recorder. It should fit so that one end of it is level with the edge of the hole **(1)**. To make it airtight rub it with beeswax. This will form a good seal when you push it in place. The block in a recorder is usually known as a 'fipple'.

To make the instrument comfortable in your mouth, gently hold it sideways in a vice. With a coping saw remove part of the end and the block **(2)**. Take it out of the vice and sand off all the rough edges. At this stage your recorder should make a sound. If not, check to see that the windway is not blocked with sawdust.

Tuning As with other wind instruments in this book, tuning is a job that must be done slowly using another instrument. On the recorder, the first stage is to saw the tube shorter until the note G is obtained. At present you should get somewhere around F sharp. You will need to saw off about 6 mm and check the pitch again. Keep doing this until you get a steady note of G. Sand the end of your recorder smooth.

The first hole is 65 mm from the open end of the recorder. Drill this out to 5 mm diameter and see what note you get. It should be near to an A. Use a small round file to open out the hole until the A is in tune **(3)**. Keep checking your work to make sure that you don't go too far when opening out the holes. If you take out too much wood, either stick a wooden plug in the hole and start to drill it out again, or partly close the hole with a few drops of wax.

All the other five holes on the recorder are drilled and tuned in the same way. Their distances from the open end are B 107 mm, C 140 mm, D 173 mm, E 208 mm, F sharp 241 mm. All of them start at 6 mm in diameter.

When all the holes are in tune the instrument can be cleaned up. Sandpaper it, round off the corners, and then give it at least two coats of varnish **4)**. To give it a stronger voice, it is a good idea to oil the inside of the tube with olive oil. This will stop moisture from your breath making the wood inside go furry and deadening the tone.

Playing the recorder Unlike the flute there is no special way to blow because the windway does it for you. The right hand is normally used for the bottom three holes and the left hand for the top three holes. To play a scale, simply lift off one finger after another starting at the bottom of the instrument. When you get to F sharp put all your fingers down again and blow harder for the top G and the notes above it.

The fingering on this is the same as on the flute in this book. It is also the same as that on the tin whistle flageolets you can buy at most music shops.

Elastic band

harp

This small instrument is very easy to·
make and has a sound all of its own.
The harp cannot be tuned to a proper
musical scale, but even so it can still be
made to play tunes, especially those
tunes that you make up yourself.

Perhaps the most important thing
about the elastic band harp is that it
shows how stringed instruments work.
All it consists of is a box, a block of
wood, and some elastic bands
stretched around the box and over the
block. When something like an elastic
band or a taut piece of string is
plucked, the sound it makes as it vi-
brates is very quiet. This is of no use for
music unless it can be made loud
enough to be heard clearly.

To make the sound louder (amplify),
the strings are passed over a block of
wood that is known as the bridge. The
bridge is fitted on a box called the
soundbox. This has some sort of hole
in it to let the sound out. Once the
string has been plucked, the vibrations
go through the bridge and make the
whole of the top of the soundbox vibrate. This greatly amplifies the sound.

All stringed instruments (except
those which are amplified electrically)
have a bridge and a soundbox with
soundholes. On a guitar the soundhole
is round, while on a violin it is 'f'-

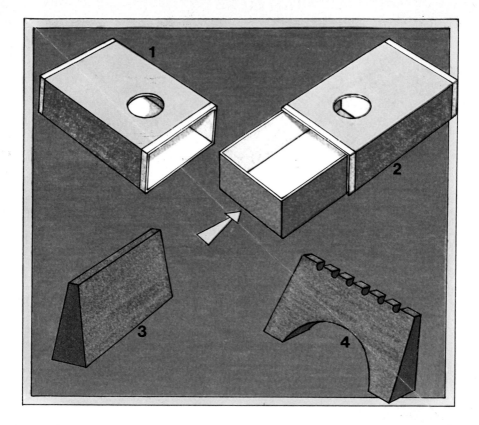

shaped. Soundholes were often made in complicated shapes and were the main point of decoration on an instrument. Have a look at some of the other string instruments in this book and see if you can see their bridges and soundboxes.

Materials, tools, and equipment
One large empty matchbox
A scrap piece of hardwood
Packet of elastic bands
Saw, knife, glue, paint

Method Take the matchbox, and using something like a sharp knife or a leather punch cut out a soundhole in one side of the box **(1)**. It doesn't matter what shape you make the hole. Your own design would make it more personal. When the soundhole is finished, glue in the tray with its bottom on the opposite side of the matchbox to the soundhole **(2)**.

Find a piece of scrap hardwood about 50 x 25 x 6 mm for the bridge. It can be cut to any shape you want or left as a rectangular block. In either case the sides should be cut away so that the block is reduced to about 3 mm in thickness **(3)**. In the top you will also need to cut a notch for each band you want to fit on your harp. The finished bridge should look like that in the drawing **(4)**.

Before you assemble your harp give the box a coat of paint to make it colourful. As soon as this is dry you can wrap it with elastic bands, fit the bridge under them and start playing. There are no playing instructions, just pluck the strings and have fun.

Try experimenting with the bridge in different positions or by using thicker or thinner elastic bands. Soon you will begin to understand all the basic scientific principles that lie behind the working of a stringed instrument.

Monochord

Materials, tools, and equipment
3 mm ply 500 × 65 mm
2 pieces pine 200 × 25 × 10 mm
2 pieces hardwood 45 × 25 mm
    square
A violin peg, No. 3 gauge music wire
Triangular moulding, drills, glue,
    wood screw
Hammer, panel pins, a round file
Masking tape

The monochord is an instrument that has only one playing string. It was originally used to work out the notes of the musical scale. A famous ancient Greek called Pythagoras was supposed to have done this work and the scale he calculated then is very similar to the ones used today. In the Middle Ages monks used the monochord to train singers. At the same time the monochord was developed into two new instruments: the hurdy-gurdy, which will be covered later, and the delicate clavichord, one of the earliest keyboard instruments.

Method Take the strips of pine and the hardwood blocks and make up a rectangular frame. Put some glue on the corners and pin them together to make a good solid joint **(1)**. When the frame is complete, glue the pieces of plywood on the top and bottom to make up a box. Use masking tape to hold it together while it dries. Once the glue has set, remove the tape. Draw a line right down the centre of the top of the monochord. At 12 mm in from one end of this line drill a 6 mm hole 22 mm deep, and 12 mm in from the other end

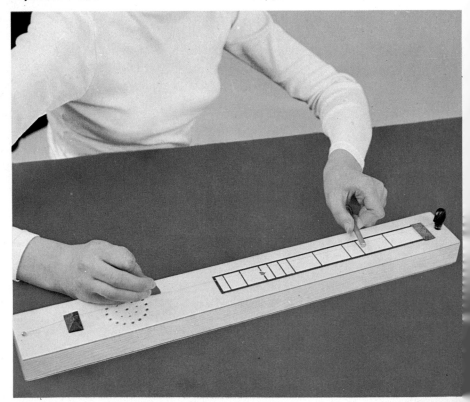

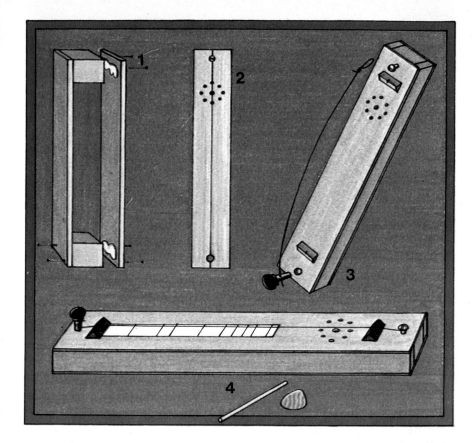

of the line drill a 3 mm hole, and partly screw in the woodscrew. Also on this centre line, about 150 mm from the screw, design and drill a rose sound-hole similar to the one used on the African sansa **(2)**.

Take a small round file and open out the top of the 6 mm hole until the violin peg fits in nice and firmly. If the hole in the peg is now below the top of the instrument, drill a new hole about 1.5 mm diameter in the top part of the peg. Saw off two 25 mm lengths of moulding for the bridges and make a small notch in the middle of the top of each. Glue on the bridges with their notches above the centre line and 50 mm in from the ends of the sound-box. Now sand down the whole box and apply at least two coats of varnish.

Make up the string from a length of music wire by twisting a loop in one end. Fit the string on the screw, over the bridges, and through the hole in the peg **(3)**. Turn the peg clockwise to tighten the string.

Perhaps the best way to play your monochord is to use a guitar plectrum and a short length of metal bar. Hold the bar on the string while you pluck it. You will find that by moving the bar along the string you will change the note. To make playing easier, stick a strip of paper on the soundboard, and then tune the string to the note C on a piano. Now play a D on the piano and slide the bar along the string until the monochord also plays a D. Mark on the paper the position of the bar, and repeat this method for the other notes in the scale **(4)**. Anyone who can play a piano will help you do this. Once the scale is marked out your monochord will play in any key that you tune it to.

Lyre

The lyre was a very popular instrument with the ancient Greeks. Competitions were often held, and the best players would have the girls in the audience screaming, just as pop stars do today. Anglo-Saxons played a less ornate type of lyre known as the rotte. One of these was found amongst the jewellery in the royal ship burial of AD 670 at Sutton Hoo. Another was found in the coffin of a 6th-century warrior buried in the Black Forest. It is on this instrument that your design is based.

Materials, tools, and equipment
Pine (body) 750 × 150 × 25 mm
Hardwood (cross bar) 150 × 40 × 25 mm
3 mm ply (soundboard) 750 × 150 mm
Six violin pegs, No. 3 gauge music wire
A piece of triangular moulding
A length of 12 mm dowel
Glue, varnish, 6 mm drill, gouge, bowsaw, spokeshave, mallet, file, screwdriver
Two ¾″ No. 8 woodscrews

Method The rotte is cut from pine hollowed out to make a soundbox. Mark out its shape on the pine, following the outline in **(1)**. Use a bowsaw to cut out the rotte, being careful not to cut inside the lines. Accurately saw halfway through both ends of the rotte and the piece of hardwood, to make the joints

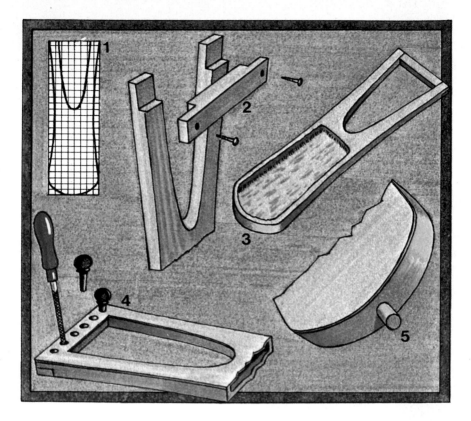

shown in **(2)**. Glue and screw the cross bar in place.

Draw a pencil line around the top of the instrument 10 mm in from the edge. This line is used as a guide for chiselling out the soundbox. Use a gouge and mallet to hollow out the rotte. Be careful not to go through the sides or back of the instrument. The inside does not need to have a perfect finish, but try and make the sides and back of the rotte about 10 mm thick **(3)**. Lay the body on the thin ply and draw around it. Cut the ply to shape. Glue it over the whole of the top of the body. When the glue has set you can shape the rotte with the spokeshave, rounding off all the edges and making sure the plywood is level with the edges of the body. Finish off the instrument with a piece of glass paper.

Along the cross bar draw a centre line and mark six places an equal distance apart for the tuning pegs. Drill six

6 mm holes right through the rotte. Carefully open out the top of the holes with a round file to get a good fit with the pegs **(4)**. Drill a 12 mm hole in the middle of the bottom edge of the instrument, and glue in a short piece of dowel so that there is still about 12 mm sticking out **(5)**. A bridge is made from 75 mm of the triangular moulding. Finish off the rotte with at least two coats of varnish applied with a cloth. When dry, sand it down with flour paper and then apply wax polish.

The strings are cut to length. One end is made into a loop that is put around the dowel, while the other end is passed over the bridge and through the hole in the peg. Probably the best tuning is the first six notes of the scale of G, these being G, A, B, C, D, and E. If you find that the pegs start slipping just push them in harder to give a better grip. To play the rotte, hold it in your left hand and pluck it like a harp.

Psaltery

The psaltery is a simple instrument, consisting of a few strings stretched across a pair of bridges on top of a soundbox. A player would place the instrument on his lap, and pluck the strings with his fingers or with a goose quill, producing a sound similar to the harp. Psalteries first appeared at the end of the 12th century, when they were made in many different shapes and sizes. Some were square, others triangular, but the most popular psalteries had a shape like that of a pig's snout. This shape can still be seen in the harpsichord, which is really a large psaltery played by a keyboard.

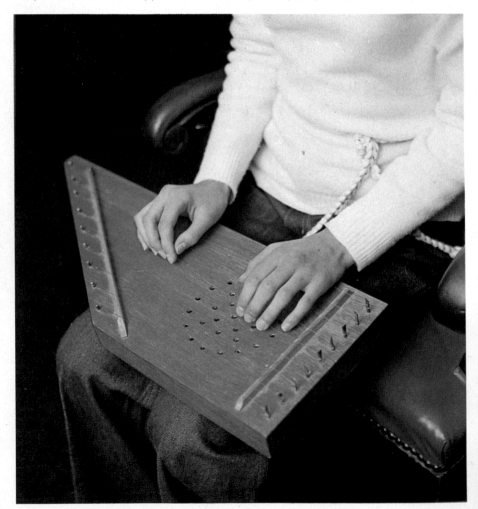

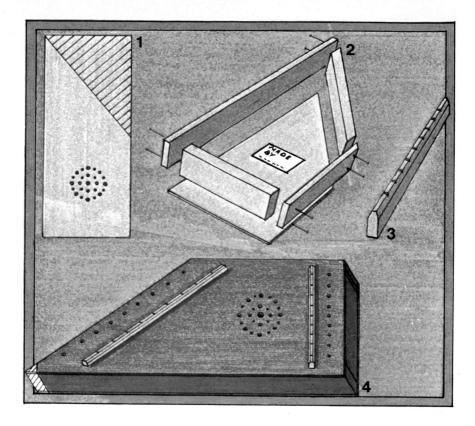

Materials, tools, and equipment

2 sheets of 3 mm ply 520 × 200 mm

Pine 800 × 50 × 10 mm

Beech (or other hardwood) 550 × 50 × 20 mm

Beech (or other hardwood) 500 × 10 × 6 mm

3 mm diameter steel rod (3″ nails)

8 mm diameter steel rod, No. 3 gauge music wire

Saws, glue, panel pins, 1 and 3 mm drills

Hammer, file, varnish, scrap of tubing

Masking tape

Method: The soundbox

Start by taking one piece of plywood, and mark the centre of one long side. Draw a line from this mark to an opposite corner, and then carefully saw along this line. Do the same with the other sheet of plywood, and then choose one to be the top or soundboard for the psaltery.

In the middle of the soundboard, design and drill out a rose as described in the construction of the sansa **(1)**.

Saw off two pieces of pine, one 520 mm and the other 270 mm long. Also saw off two lengths of beech, one 180 mm and the other 330 mm long. Take the shortest pieces of pine and beech and glue the pine onto the end of the beech so that they form a right angle. When you are sure it is correct, hammer in two panel pins to complete the joint. Do the same with the second piece of pine, but on the other end of the block of beech, making sure both pieces are pointing in the same direction. Once the glue has set the assembly can be glued onto the plywood back. Use tape to hold the wood while the glue dries. The remaining piece of beech has now to be cut to fit along the sloping side of the frame. To do this, put the wood in position, and mark on it

49

where it has to be cut. Carefully saw along these marks, and then glue and pin the block in place. Write out your maker's label and glue this inside the box, which should now look like **(2)**.

Saw off two pieces of beech for the bridges, one 180 mm and the other 320 mm long. Hold the wood in a vice and file away the corners on the top edges of both pieces. Mark the centre on each bridge. Make four other marks on either side 22 mm apart on the short bridge, and 38 mm apart on the longer bridge. Cut small notches on the tops of the bridges at these positions **(3)**.

Glue the soundboard on the psaltery, and then sand down the completed box when the glue has set. Next glue on the two bridges so that they are both 35 mm in from the edges of the box. Behind each bridge and 6 mm in from the edges of the box, drill nine 3 mm holes about 20 mm deep. Each hole should be in line with a notch on the bridge **(4)**. One or two coats of varnish will complete the soundbox.

Tuning the psaltery

The tuning and hitch pins Both the tuning pins and the hitch pins are made from 3 mm mild steel rod. If you are unable to get this you can use ordinary 3″ round nails with the heads and points sawn off. For the tuning pins saw off nine 40 mm lengths, and remove the sharp corners with a file. Using a hammer and a solid object such as an anvil, flatten out one end of each pin so that it is 8 mm wide **(1)**. Be careful not to hit your fingers with the hammer. Drill a 1 mm hole through each pin 15 mm from the flattened end **(2)** and the tuning pins are complete.

To make the hitch pins saw off nine 25 mm lengths of steel rod, and remove the sharp edges with a file. Carefully saw half-way through each pin 3 mm from one end, and then the hitch pins are complete **(3)**. Gently hammer the tuning and hitch pins into their holes in the soundbox. The tuning pins fit along the square end of the instrument and are driven in so their holes lie 3 mm above the soundboard. Drive the hitch pins in along the sloping edge until their notches are also 3 mm above the soundboard.

The strings On this psaltery the strings are all of the same thickness (gauge), and can easily be made up from lengths of music wire. To do this cut nine 600 mm lengths of wire, and at one end of each make a loop by bending the wire back and twisting it together **(4)**. This should be done with a pair of pliers as the ends of the wire can be sharp.

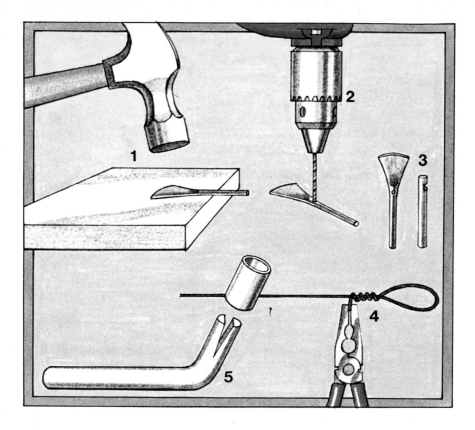

Tuning key A key has to be made to turn the tuning pins before the strings can be fitted. Make this from 100 mm of 8 mm diameter steel bar, and start by sawing a V-shaped slot 20 mm deep in one end. With one end of the rod held firmly in a vice, hammer the other end of the rod until it is almost bent to a right angle. Now saw off 25 mm of metal tubing that will be a tight fit on the rod, and push it on over the slotted end of the key **(5)**. Remove any sharp edges with a file and the tuning key is ready to use.

Tuning To fit a string, put the loop over the hitch pin and into the notch, and then pass the other end of the string through the hole in the tuning pin. Slot the tuning key on top of the tuning pin, and wind up the string clockwise. Make sure that as the string gets tight it is put in the correct notches on the bridges. Use the same method to put on all nine strings. Any extra wire sticking out from the tuning pins can now be cut off with wire cutters.

Perhaps the best way to tune your psaltery is to find someone who has a piano or recorder, and who can play you the notes of the scale of G major. The bottom note (the longest string) is tuned to G, and the rest of the strings are tuned to the other notes of the scale ending with an A. Use the tuning key to tighten or slacken the string until it sounds the same as the note on the piano. Tuning is not easy if you are not used to it, but after a time you will find it can be done without listening to another instrument. At last your psaltery is finished and ready to be played.

Fiddle

This fiddle is made to look like those used five hundred years ago by musicians at the royal courts of Europe. Its construction is not traditional but has been simplified so that it is easy to make. It uses violin strings (gut), and tuning pegs. Although this design has five strings you could make it with only three or four if you prefer. Before you start, read through all the instructions so that you can understand how it is put together. Don't rush, an instrument

like this will take a long time to make well.

Materials, tools, and equipment
Pine block (body) 275 × 150 × 37 mm
3 mm ply (soundboard) 275 × 150 mm
Strips of beech (or other hardwood)
   (Neck) 550 × 75 × 13 mm
   (Fingerboard) 200 × 50 × 13 mm
   (Tailpiece) 125 × 50 × 10 mm
   (Bridge) 50 × 50 × 10 mm
10 mm dowel, bowsaw, gouge, mallet,
   glue, drills, chisel, plane, varnish
Five violin pegs, a set of gut violin
   strings and a gut viola C string

Method: The body and neck Start by drawing the outline of the body on the block of pine **(1)**. To make this easier use a sheet of paper the same size, and fold it in half along its length. Cut out half the shape with scissors so that when the paper is opened out it can be

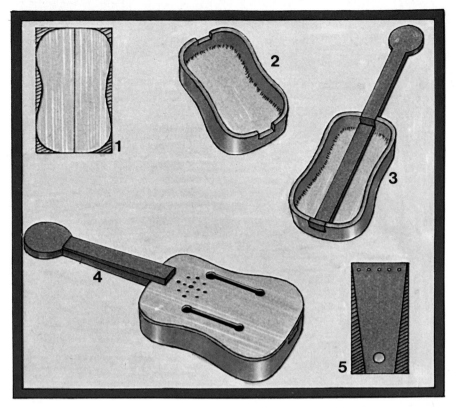

used as a pattern. Mark out and saw the block to shape. Draw a line 13 mm from the edge around the top of the block, and use this as a guide to gouge out all the wood from the centre. Use the gouge and mallet, and be careful not to go through the sides or back of the block. Make two saw cuts 13 mm deep, 25 mm either side of the centre at the ends of the block, and then chisel out the wood in between **(2)**.

Make the neck out of the long strip of hardwood by first marking out its shape. This consists of a 75 mm circular shape at one end, with the rest sawn down to 50 mm wide so that it fits into the slots in the body. With the neck in place, mark where the inside edges of the body come to, then remove the neck and cut the wood down to 8 mm thick between the lines **(3)**. Now you can glue the neck to the body.

Use the paper pattern for the shape of the soundboard and cut it out from the thin plywood. If you want a rose

soundhole like the psaltery, drill this out now. Early fiddles often had two slots in the soundboard to let the sound out. Try not to cut too much out from the soundboard. If you do you will need to glue wooden struts underneath to strengthen it. When this is done, glue the soundboard in place.

The fingerboard is cut from a second strip of hardwood, and is shaped to fit on the neck, with one end at the edge of the circle. Plane the neck so that it tapers evenly to 3 mm over its length and then glue it in place **(4)**.

A piece of wood called the tailpiece is cut from hardwood and is used to anchor the strings. It has five 1.5 mm holes along its top edge, and a 13 mm hole at the bottom to attach it to the body **(5)**.

Drill five 6 mm holes in the end of the neck in the shape of a five on a dice. With a round file open out these holes until the violin pegs fit firmly. Sand down the whole instrument.

Fiddle

fitting the

strings

tuning

Fitting the strings At this stage your basic fiddle is complete, and what remains to be done is the fitting and adjusting of the strings.

Start by making the peg on which the tailpiece is hooked. This is best made from a short piece of 10 mm dowel and cut to the shape in **(1)**. A 10 mm hole is then drilled in the end of the fiddle, and the peg is glued in place with the notch above the soundboard, and facing away from the tuning pegs. Next saw out the bridge from a piece of 10 mm hardwood to the shape shown in **(2)**. Notice that the bridge should be thinner at the top than at the bottom, and do not shape the top of the bridge until later.

At the other end of the instrument is another small bridge called the nut. This is made from a scrap of hardwood the size of a matchstick, and glued at the end of the fingerboard **(3)**. Make a small notch in the centre of the top of the nut, and then make two others on each side, 11 mm apart, for the strings. To keep the strings on the nut, a length of 3 mm wire is bent to the shape shown in **(3)** and pushed into two 3 mm holes drilled in the neck. Leave enough room for the strings to pass underneath.

Hook the tailpiece in position and tie on the middle string. Pass the other

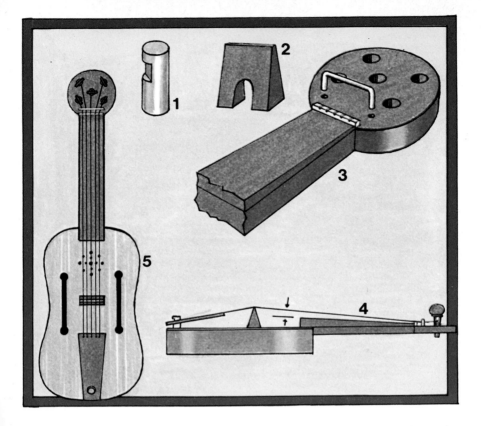

end of the string over the bridge and over the nut, under the metal bridge, and through the hole in the middle peg. Tighten the string so that the bridge is 300 mm away from the nut. Carefully cut a notch in the middle of the bridge, deep enough so that the string lies about 5 mm above the thick end of the fingerboard (4). This process (known as 'adjusting the action') is important, as it will determine how easy the fiddle is to play. Make two more notches in the bridge 11 mm either side of the centre, and adjust the action so that the next two strings are 4 mm above the thick end of the fingerboard. Finally add another two notches to the bridge 11 mm out from the last two, and set these outer strings so that they are 3 mm above the end of the fingerboard. The reason the strings are at different heights is so they can be bowed one at a time, which would not be possible if the bridge were flat.

Remove the strings and shape the top of the bridge to a curve, leaving the notches deep enough to hold the strings. Lightly sand down the fiddle again, and apply at least two coats of varnish to seal the wood.

Tuning Violin strings are fitted and tuned from right to left (5) to E, A, D, and G. The fifth is a gut viola string tuned to C. If you want your fiddle with four strings leave off the C, and if you want only three strings also leave off the top E string. Remember, if you use fewer strings, to space them further apart on the bridge and nut.

A friend who can play the notes on a piano can help you tune the fiddle, but you really need a teacher to show you how to play it, unless you can already play a violin. Fiddles are played in the same way as violins, but they are usually held in the crook of your arm instead of under your chin.

55

TO22094

Fiddle bow

You can always use a modern bow to play your fiddle, but it will not look right with the instrument. Early bows were often shorter, had less hair than nowadays, and the hair was usually black. There were also many different types of bow. Some looked like the type of bow that would fire an arrow, while others were straight sticks on which the hair was pulled tight by the player's hand. The bow described below is made from a straight stick with a block of wood known as the frog, which is used to tighten the hairs. It is a fairly common design from the 15th century. Hanks of horse hair for bows can be obtained from music shops. Black and white hair is available, as well as a synthetic substitute that can also be used.

Materials, tools, and equipment
Hardwood 600 × 10 × 6 mm
Hardwood 40 × 25 × 10 mm
Hank of horse hair (preferably black)
Coping saw, chisel, drill, varnish,
 rosin

Method Take the long strip of wood and draw lines across at 75 mm and 115 mm from one end. Make saw cuts 2 mm deep right across the bow on these lines, and then gently chisel out

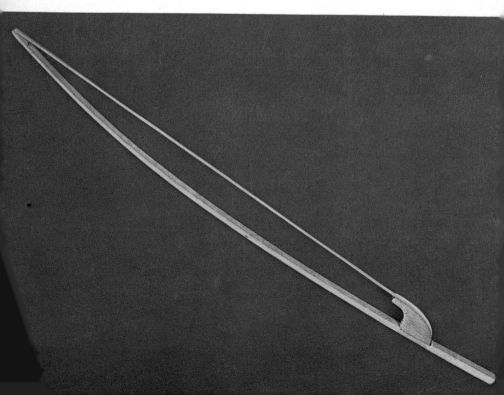

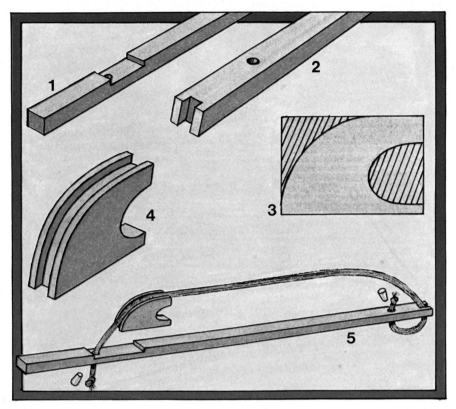

the wood in between these cuts to make a recess **(1)**. Drill a 3 mm hole at the end of the recess nearest the end of the bow. Next work on the other end of the bow by sawing down 3 mm at 2 mm in from each side, and then chiselling out the wood in between **(2)**. Measure 25 mm from this end of the bow and drill another 3 mm hole right through.

To make the frog for your bow, first saw the hardwood block to the shape shown in **(3)**. Very carefully chisel a channel 6 mm wide and 3 mm deep around the top edge of the frog, using a 6 mm chisel **(4)**. Take your time making the frog because it is easy to slip and make a mistake.

The hair can now be fitted, but before you start to do this make two little wedges of wood that are a tight fit in the holes in the bow. Keep these safe as you will need them later. Tie a knot at one end of the hank of hair, and pass the rest of the hair through the hole at the notched end of the bow, so that the knot ends up on the same side as the recess **(5)**. Glue, and drive in one wedge to hold the hair in place; be careful not to split the bow. Comb out the hair to make sure it is not twisted, and then pass it through the hole in the recess. Now tie a knot at the end of the hank of hair, and clip the frog in place. Pass the hair round the channel in the frog, pulling it as tight as you can with the knot, and while it is like this glue and drive in the second wedge. Remove the frog while the glue dries. Once the glue has set, replace the frog. Trim off the excess hair and the ends of the wedges and sand down the bow. Apply two coats of varnish, being careful not to get any varnish on the horse hair.

Your bow is now complete, but before it will work the hair needs to be rubbed on a block of rosin to make it sticky, so that it will play the strings.

Hurdy-gurdy

The hurdy-gurdy is an ancient instrument that sounds rather like bagpipes, and is great fun to play. It is also a solo instrument because it accompanies itself with a drone. Some of its history is given in the introduction to this book.

Materials, tools, and equipment
Two pieces 3 mm ply 460 × 216 mm
Two 9 mm pine sides 460 × 75 mm
Block of beech 215 × 75 × 19 mm
Some beech 12 mm thick for the
   pegbox
Some beech 6 mm thick for the
   tangent box
10 mm square beech for the keys

12 mm ply for the wheel, a scrap of
   1 mm ply
Some triangular moulding, 3 violin
   pegs
6 mm steel rod 280 mm long, washers
Gut violin A string, gut viola C and D
   strings, 2 guitar buttons and a strap
Other equipment as for the psaltery

Method: The body and pegbox
Begin by marking out the shape of the soundboard and the back on the 3 mm ply. Do this by measuring 53 mm from each corner on one of the short edges, and drawing from these points to the top corners **(1)**. Mark out both pieces and saw them to shape. The sound-board will need a 120 × 40 mm slot cut from it, with the top edge 100 mm from the wide end of the board. First draw its outline with a pencil. Drill a 6 mm hole at each corner, and then saw it out with a coping saw. If you wish to have a rose soundhole drill this out now **(1)**; details are given in the instructions for the

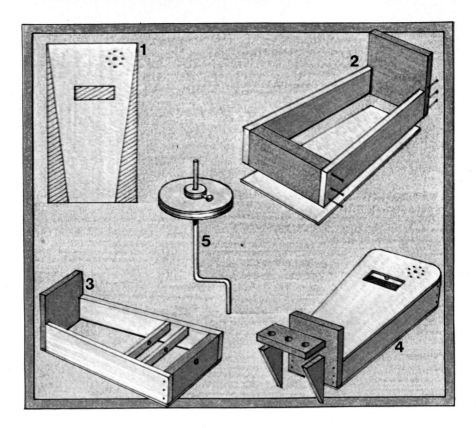

sansa.

Make the ends of the beech block the same angle as the sides of the sound-board. Saw the pegbox end from 12 mm beech 120 × 110 mm. Next glue and pin the pine sides to the beech block and to the end, then glue the assembly onto the ply back and let it set **(2)**. Measure 90 mm and 145 mm from the wide end. Saw off two lengths of 12 × 9 mm wood to fit across the inside of the body at these positions. Before you glue these struts in place, drill a 6 mm hole through the middle of each, and also through the centre of the beech block 6 mm down from the top. Glue in the struts **(3)**, then the soundboard. When it is dry round off the widest corners with a file.

Make up the pegbox from two pieces of 12 mm beech 110 × 50 mm. Saw one piece from corner to corner to make two triangles, and drill three 6 mm holes in the remaining piece 30 mm

apart, for the tuning pegs. Now glue these pieces to the end of the body, using tape to hold it while it dries **(4)**.

The wheel The wheel is a disc of 12 mm ply 90 mm diameter. It is drawn with a compass, carefully sawn out, and then has a 6 mm hole drilled in the middle. Another disc of 12 mm ply 25 mm diameter is drilled and glued to the larger disc so that their holes line up. Your wheel must be perfectly round, so ask someone who has the use of a machine called a lathe to trim it up for you. A woodscrew through the smaller disc will hold the wheel on the axle **(5)**. The axle is made from 280 mm of 6 mm steel rod. This is bent in a vice 50 mm and 100 mm from one end to form the handle. Fit the axle through the body. Add the wheel with some washers either side to prevent it from moving. Tighten the screw onto the axle.

Hurdy-gurdy

tangent box

and keys

The tangent box, and keys This is made from four strips of 6 mm beech, two pieces 320 × 32 mm and two others 320 × 10 mm. Eight notches have to be accurately cut from the wider strips **(1)**. It is important that they are in the right place or the instrument will not play in tune. Mark the end of one piece of wood, and from it measure the following distances, drawing pencil lines across the top edge: 41 mm, 77 mm, 95 mm, 126 mm, 152 mm, 167 mm, 187 mm, and 210 mm. Measure 5 mm either side of these marks, and saw down 10 mm on these new lines. Then with a sharp chisel chop out the wood in between the cuts, leaving a square notch. You will find it easier if you place one piece of wood behind the other and cut out both at once. Use a piece of 10 mm square wood to test that it fits accurately into each notch **(1)**. The narrow strips are now glued on top of the notched edges to form square holes. Saw off two pieces of 6 mm beech 40 × 32 mm. Glue these pieces together with the sides you have just made to form a

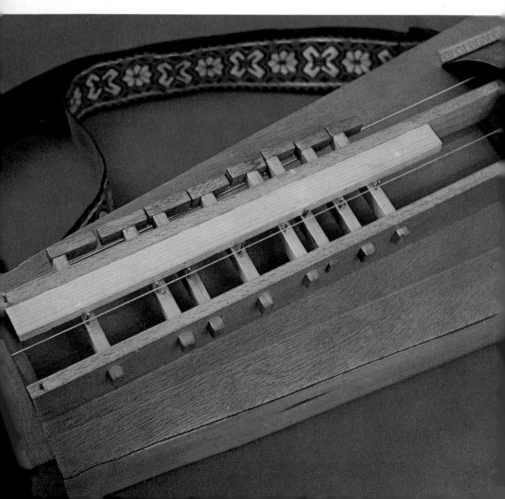

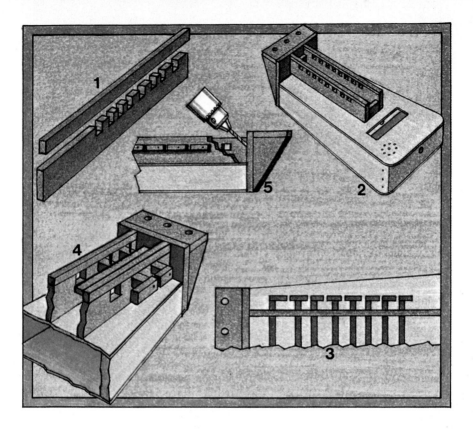

box. Glue the box onto the sound-board, with the end you marked earlier up against the pegbox **(2)**.

Saw off eight pieces of 10 mm square wood 75 mm long, three pieces 25 mm long, two pieces 23 mm long, and three more pieces 20 mm long. These will make the keys. The long strips of wood slide through the square holes, and the smaller strips are pinned and glued to one end. Your fingers will operate these keys. The 20 mm pieces are used for the three keys nearest the wheel, while the 25 mm pieces are used for the keys at the pegbox end. Look at **(3)** and notice how these are fitted. Fit them one at a time, and make sure that they do not touch or jam. Now drill a 1 mm hole in the middle of the top of each sliding key and with the keys in the box drive in ½" panel pins, leaving them sticking up 7 mm. Check that these pins are at the same distances from the pegbox as were the notches in the

tangent box sides. If some are out of position then either bend them back, or remove them and put in a new pin. Along the keyed side of the box, glue to the top of the inside a strip of 6 mm wood 200 × 16 mm **(4)**.

In the centre of the front of the pegbox, and 36 mm up from the sound-board, drill a 3 mm hole that is angled downwards **(5)**. Drill another 3 mm hole on each side of the pegbox front 15 mm in from the edge and up from the soundboard.

A lid for the tangent box can be cut from 6 mm wood 320 × 52 mm. Hold it in place on the instrument, and drill a 1 mm hole through each corner and into the wood underneath. Remove the lid and open out the holes in it to 1.5 mm. Now replace it, and drive in four panel pins that have had their heads filed off. Stop when they are flush with the top of the lid. These will act as pegs for the lid to fit on.

Hurdy-gurdy

fitting strings

Fitting the strings Start the final stage of your hurdy-gurdy by drilling two 6 mm holes in the soundboard 25 mm from the widest end and 45 mm either side of the centre. With a small knife cut these to the shape shown in **(1)**, then cut two 19 mm lengths of triangular moulding.

The drone strings (viola D and C) are now fitted as follows. First tie a knot in one end, and put this through the shaped hole, pulling it into the narrow part so that the knot becomes trapped. Second, pass the other end of the string through the hole in the pegbox and the peg. Now turn the peg and tighten the string. Use the moulding as a bridge by gluing it to the soundboard about 40 mm from the wheel **(2)**. Move the string along the bridge until it touches the wheel. Mark this point on the bridge and notch it for the string. If you rub some rosin onto the wheel, and wrap a little cotton wool around the string where it touches the wheel, you should eventually get a good steady note from each string when the wheel is turned.

A tailpiece is cut from 6 mm beech 65 × 25 mm. One end has a 1.5 mm hole in the centre, and the other end is filed at an angle, and fixed to the instrument with two screws **(3)**. The main bridge is cut to the shape in **(4)** from 10 mm hardwood 38 mm square. It should also be made to taper so the top is only

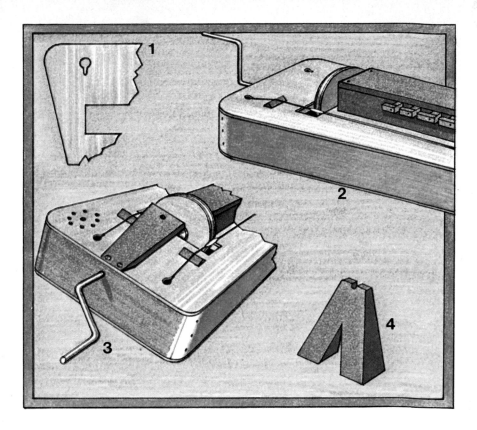

3 mm thick. Now it can be glued in place in the centre of the soundboard and exactly 377 mm from the front of the pegbox.

To fit the main playing string (violin A), knot one end, and pass the other through the hole in the tailpiece from underneath. Take the other end and feed it through the pegbox and the middle peg, then tighten the string, making sure it is on the bridge. Carefully notch the centre of the bridge until the string rubs on the wheel. Add some cotton wool, and adjust the string until you get a clear, steady tone. Finally glue a 65 mm strip of moulding along the edges of the wheel slot, and when they are dry, clip in a piece of 1 mm ply 190 × 65 mm to act as a cover.

Tuning and playing Fit a guitar button on each end of your instrument for the strap, which is fastened around your back. Hold the hurdy-gurdy at an angle on your lap so that the keys fall away from the string. Now, with the drone strings removed from their notches, only the melody string should sound, and this is tuned to G. It should now be possible to play a scale by pressing the keys. From the pegbox end the keys should give the following notes: A, B, C, D, E, F, G, and A. Check that the keys all slide easily and that none stick when they are pressed against the string. If the sound is not even then the wheel is probably not round, and it will need to be trued up and sanded smooth on a lathe.

Wind the handle with your right hand, and play the keys with your left. The third key gives C, and this is the note both drones are tuned to, one being an octave below the other. Use one or both drones when playing your hurdy-gurdy, and you will find that it can make a really good sound. Give it a coat of varnish to finish it off.

Conversion table	
millimetres (mm)	inches (in)
3	⅛
6	¼
13	½
19	¾
25	1
38	1½
44	1¾
51	2
64	2½
76	3
89	3½
102	4
127	5
152	6
178	7
203	8
229	9
254	10
381	15
508	20
635	25
762	30
889	35

Acknowledgments.

The author would like to express his gratitude to the following people for their encouragement and help in compiling this book.

To Janet Allison, Jane Burkinshaw, Angela Makey, Suzanne Roscow, Sally Crowson, and Debbie Castledine, who are all pupils at the Waltham Toll Bar School near Grimsby. These young people form the nucleus of the Toll Bar Consort, a music group that concentrates on the performance of medieval and Renaissance music. Having made several of their own instruments, they agreed to be photographed with them for the book.

Appreciation is also extended to members of staff at the school, especially in the practical and music departments, for the use of their facilities and above all for their tolerance.

Finally thanks to the author's wife for her patience, and to John Evans for supplying the copper tubing.

Picture on page 7 supplied by the Mansell Collection.